X-TREME OUTDOORS

ROCK CLIMBING

AILEEN WEINTRAUB

HIGH interest **books**

Children's Press®
A Division of Scholastic Inc.
New York / Toronto / London / Auckland / Sydney
Mexico City / New Delhi / Hong Kong
Danbury, Connecticut

Book Design: Michael DeLisio
Contributing Editor: M.B. Pitt
Photo Credits: Cover © Corey Rich/Icon SMI; title page, p. 3 © Corbis; p. 5
© Todd Powell/Index Stock Imagery, Inc.; p. 6 © Benelux Press/Index Stock
Imagery, Inc.; p. 9 © Mark Hunt/Index Stock Imagery, Inc.; pp. 11, 13, 18, 24,
26, 32, 40 © Greg Epperson/Index Stock Imagery, Inc.; p. 14 © Michael
Brinson/Index Stock Imagery, Inc.; p. 16 © Tim Lynch/Index Stock Imagery,
Inc.; p. 21, back cover © Duomo/Corbis; pp. 23, 28 © Galen Rowell/Corbis;
p. 31 © Jim McGuire/Index Stock Imagery, Inc.; p. 35 © Wolfgang Kaehler/
Corbis; p. 36 © Karl Weatherly/Corbis; p. 38 © Joseph Sohm; ChromoSohm
Inc./Corbis

Library of Congress Cataloging-in-Publication Data

Weintraub, Aileen, 1973-
  Rock climbing / Aileen Weintraub.
  p. cm. — (X-treme outdoors)
  Includes index.
  Summary: Discusses the skills and equipment needed for rock climbing,
  climbing techniques, safety concerns, and places to climb.
  ISBN 0-516-24319-5 (lib. bdg.) — ISBN 0-516-24381-0 (pbk.)
  1. Rock climbing—Juvenile literature. [1. Rock climbing.] I. Title.
  II. Series.

  GV200.2 .W45 2003
  796.52'23—dc21

                                                    2002011243

CONTENTS

INTRODUCTION

The blazing sun beats down on your forehead. You can feel beads of sweat trickling down your arms. You want to brush the sweat aside, but you don't dare move your hands. Both of your hands are clinging to a giant, sheer slab of granite rock. You are hanging 80 feet (24.4 meters) in the air on a steep crag, or chunk of rock. You have got to keep your mind on only one thing—your next move. A slight breeze offers relief from the heat. You finally make a decision. Your hands reach for a small knob in the crack of the rock. Now you're one small step closer to your goal.

There's nothing like conquering a mountain. Climbing to the top, inch by grueling inch, gives you a sense of pride. In the last few years, the popularity of rock climbing has scaled to new heights. For many, the thrill of climbing a wall of rock is irresistible. People refer to rock climbing as an *X-treme* sport. *X-treme* sports appeal to people who like to test their physical limits. Like other *X-treme* sports, rock climbing

The *X-treme* sport of rock climbing demands intense concentration and patience.

focuses on individual challenges, and individual achievement. Climbs may take you thousands of feet upward. However, some of the most difficult climbs can be a mere 40 feet (12.2 m) long.

Climbers must be disciplined and patient. They are taking on the toughest challenges nature has to offer. Once they get to the top of a mountain, though, climbers get their reward. The view makes all that effort worthwhile. Sound like your kind of sport? If so, turn the pages and see the sights!

CHAPTER ONE

FIRST STEPS

There's no way to be certain who climbed the first mountain for fun, or when it happened. We do know that by the 1850s, rock climbing was beginning to be considered a social event. That was when the first climbing club was formed.

Mountaineering first became popular in Europe. In the 1930s, Americans began to get involved in the sport. At this time, many American families had begun living in large cities. These large urban centers were often far from any wilderness. As automobiles became affordable, however, families were able to drive to out-of-the-way places. People living in large cities could escape the smoggy, crowded streets, and drive to a peaceful setting. The lure of mountain views and clean air appealed greatly to these people.

Scaling rocks and mountains may be an *X-treme* sport, but it's not a brand-new one, as this vintage photo proves.

After conquering American peaks, such as Mount Owen in Wyoming, climbers began seeking more exotic adventures. They scaled mountains in the Himalayas and the Andes. They were pushing themselves to new limits. As they did, the thrills—and dangers—reached new heights.

GET FIT

Not so long ago, rock climbing was considered to be a man's sport. Now, more and more women participate. With the right attitude, anyone can climb.

You will need to be in good shape. Still, you don't have to be able to move mountains in order to climb them. Technique and style are much more important than brute strength. Don't be surprised, however, if your first few climbs lead to soreness the morning after. Strenuous rock climbing works muscles you may not even realize you have. You'll probably feel the aches all over—in your forearms, hands, triceps, biceps, shoulders, back, and abdomen.

Before your first climb, start a cross-training regimen. Cross-training activities include running, lifting weights, and cycling. These activities all help build a

It's technique, not brute strength, that allows rock climbers to face and conquer the challenges of their sport.

basic level of fitness. Not only do climbers have to be strong enough to lift their own weight, but they often have to carry a lot of gear. Being in shape beforehand will save precious energy when you're lugging all that stuff around.

Of course, it's important to remember not to overstrain. Climbers are at high risk for dislocating joints and tearing ligaments. Stretch well before each climb.

ON THE ROAD

Rock climbing is, for the most part, an outdoor sport. This means that the weather has to be just right. Warm, dry days are ideal for climbing. Rainfall makes rocks slippery—and very dangerous. Elemental forces, such as lightning or high winds, can be deadly.

Of course, not everyone lives next to a mountain. Climbers who don't live near mountains may have to travel to reach one. If you're willing to do a little research and explore new areas, however, you'll probably find a great place to climb, no matter where you live.

X-FACTOR

Do you have a tennis ball in the house? If so, then you already own one of the most powerful training tools for climbing. Just squeeze the ball in your palm over and over in your spare time. This exercise helps improve your grip. It strengthens muscles in your hands and forearms.

Many climbers turn their sport into a family affair. This father teaches his sons the ropes of rock climbing.

RISKY BUSINESS

Rock climbers must make responsible, mature decisions during their adventures. These decisions start with prevention and preparedness. Bringing the right equipment on a climb is crucial. You also need to use common sense. For instance, learn to identify plants you will want to avoid. Poison oak and poison ivy are good examples of such plants. They are often found at the bottom of crags.

BETTER SAFE THAN SORRY

It's always a good idea to carry a first aid kit. Here are items that will make your kit complete:

- Bandages
- Tweezers
- Athletic tape
- Wound cleanser
- Blister repair kit
- Antibiotic ointment
- Sunscreen
- Camping knife

Rock climbers often find themselves far away from civilization. It's important that they carry along proper equipment and first aid supplies.

CHAPTER TWO

GET IN GEAR

BOULDER DASH

Bouldering is the most basic form of rock climbing. It's also the least dangerous. Climbers stay fairly close to the ground when bouldering. No rope or gear is needed. All you need are a good pair of rock climbing shoes and a bit of gymnast's chalk. The chalk helps you keep your grip while climbing. Climbers usually hold chalk in a bag kept around their waists. Bouldering lets a climber try out difficult moves in a less dangerous setting. It also helps climbers learn to stay focused and balanced.

ROCK STARS

Once climbers get good at bouldering, they may want to tackle steeper crags. A good rope and the proper

As with other sports, amateur rock climbers should start small. They can aim for higher ground after they have a few climbs under their belts.

gear are required for these more challenging climbs. To conquer a tall mountain, climbers also need a little help from their friends.

Although you make your own moves during a climb, rock climbers are never alone. They always have a partner watching from the ground. This partner, called the belayer, is responsible for the climber's safety. The word *belay* means to make someone or something safe and secure. To successfully scale a crag, good climbers must know how to use their gear and work well with their partner.

As climbers inch slowly up the mountain, they wear a harness tied snugly around their waist. This harness holds the gear climbers need for their journey. One end of the rope is tied through the climber's harness. As the climber moves upward, he or she uses an anchor system. Anchor systems are used to attach the rope to several secure points along the climb. In other words, the climber anchors their rope to solid objects, such as large trees or boulders.

Sometimes, however, natural anchors aren't available. If that's the case, climbers have a backup option. They always bring mechanical anchors with them on

There are a few essential pieces of gear every climber should carry. The cost of these items, however, doesn't have to be steep.

Should this climber fall, he would rely on his belayer to save him from injury, or even death.

the climb. Climbers wedge these anchors into cracks in the rock. The climbers attach their end of the rope to the anchors with carabiners. Carabiners are aluminum snap-links, which connect equipment to the climbing gear.

Meanwhile, the climber's belayer is standing on the ground, holding onto the other end of the rope. He or she secures and manages this rope as the climber scales the mountain. What if the climber slips or falls? The belayer then becomes the climber's safety net. In the event of a fall, belayers apply a braking force to their end of rope. This force ensures that the anchor system will catch the falling climber.

Just like climbers, belayers must maintain constant alertness. If a climber does fall, quick, forceful action on the part of the belayer is critical. Should the belayer hesitate or become distracted, it could mean disaster for the climber.

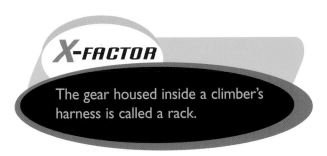

X-FACTOR

The gear housed inside a climber's harness is called a rack.

DID YOU CATCH THAT?

Sometimes it's hard for the climber and belayer to hear one another. Rock climbing is a sport in which good communication can mean the difference between life and death. To make communication easy, climbers have created commands they shout to one another. The following are some of the most common commands climbers use.

- *On belay* Belayers shout this when they're ready to accept responsibility for the climber.
- *Climbing* The climbers call this when they are ready to climb.
- *Climb* Belayers say this to signal the climbers that they can start climbing.
- *Watch me* This command alerts belayers that the climber is worried about falling.
- *Rock* This call means: "Loose rock is falling—watch out!"

THE RIGHT STUFF

Once you start tackling steeper, tougher crags, you will need more equipment. If you do not choose and use the right gear, you're asking for trouble. Rock climbing gear can be expensive, but don't worry. You don't have to buy all the gear at once. You can start off with shoes and a harness. Since your partner will have more experience than you, he or she will probably own more gear. You can borrow your partner's gear while you climb.

The rest of this chapter describes which features you should look for when you shop for gear. Keep in

Picking a comfortable, high-quality shoe will greatly assist you in your rock climbing feats.

mind, though—just having the gear won't keep you safe. You must learn how to use it correctly.

IT MUST BE THE SHOES

The right shoes are incredibly important to a great climbing experience. Most climbing shoes are made of leather. Some shoes come with lining. Don't make the mistake of picking shoes just because they look great. The most important factor is comfort. Try on several different styles and sizes to find the best fit. An all-around shoe will most likely have a medium-stiff mid-sole with low ankles. All climbing shoes have sticky rubber soles. This type of sole makes it easier to stand on thin mountain ledges.

HARNESS

Use a light harness, if possible. The leg loops should fit loosely around your thighs. Each harness has a belt to secure around the climber's waist. This belt should be long enough to double back through the buckle. Standard harness features include a belay loop, a haul loop, padding, and reinforced gear slings.

ROPE

The rope is your main source of protection. Never risk buying a used rope just to save a few dollars. When buying a rope, look on the label to see the number of test falls held, the impact force, the water repellency, and the weight. Rope should always meet high strength standards.

Always keep your rope in mint condition between climbs. After a climb, be sure to store your rope in a rope bag. This will protect it from being stepped on, and from damaging elements such as dirt, water, and extreme temperatures. Before any climb, check your rope for any signs of damage or wear.

You only want to buy a rope that is brand new. After all, it's a climber's only lifeline.

BELAY DEVICES

A belay device should be easy to use. It's crucial that the rope be able to run and slide smoothly through the belay device. This allows the belayer to pay attention to the climber without worrying about twisted rope. As you know, both the belay device and the rope keep climbers from crashing to the ground. Be sure to test the type of rope you use with any belay device you're thinking of buying. Make sure the rope slides through it easily.

CLOTHING

Climbers need to wear clothing that allows them a range of motion. On the other hand, very loose clothing can get caught in gear. Most people climb in T-shirts, spandex tights, and shorts. It's a good idea to wear long pants when climbing on rough terrain. This will protect you from getting cut or scratched.

Keep a checklist of all your gear handy. This way, you'll leave your house knowing you've got everything you need to have a great climbing day.

Remember to double-check and test your gear before each climbing expedition. You don't want to take any unnecessary risks.

CHAPTER THREE

SLEEK TECHNIQUES

Decide ahead of time, with your partner, what you both hope to accomplish on a rock climbing excursion. Set reasonable goals that match your skills.

Climbing difficulty is often rated by the following classes. The higher the number, the more advanced the climb.

Class 1 Walking or hiking across flat terrain

Class 2 Hiking across varied terrain; includes forests, fields, and small hills

Class 3 Scrambling over steep terrain; climbing that doesn't require a rope

Class 4 Climbing that requires a lot of hand and arm support; equipment is often needed

Class 5 Technical climbing; equipment is always needed for safety

Class 6 Climbing that requires pulling on a rope or standing on devices placed in the rock

With each passing year, more and more women are tackling X-treme sports.

Always be sure your first climbing partner is experienced, patient, and trustworthy.

ROCKY ROAD

It's important to be able to trust your partner. Sometimes, experienced partners may try to push novices into trying routes and crags that are beyond their skill level. An important part of climbing, of course, is pushing your limits. Only you can decide what your limits are, however. Never allow yourself to be pushed into climbing a route you think is beyond your skill. If you aren't careful, you'll find yourself facing more than you can handle.

For example, you may climb a slope that's nearly vertical. The crag only has a few small holds for your hands and feet. You struggle to take another step. You find yourself short of breath, but your partner is egging you on. "Just a little bit further!" he yells from below. You're exhausted, yet you don't want to disappoint him. You grip the next hold above you. Suddenly, it feels like your fingers have gone numb. You're out of energy and you can't hang on. You have to let go. You yell, "Falling!" to your partner and release your fingers.

Hopefully, your partner is a great belayer, and will quickly apply that braking force to catch you. Still, it's a horrific experience to have to go through. It's also one that is easily avoided, if you remember to set your limits wisely.

TRICKS OF THE TRADE

While just about anyone can climb, it takes practice to excel. Here are some techniques that skilled climbers use during their journeys.

Climbers strive to maintain three points of contact with the rock at all times. In other words, they move only one hand or foot at a time. This allows them to maintain balance at all times. On basic routes, using this strategy isn't a problem. On more difficult routes, though, it may not be so easy. Chances are your legs are stronger than your arms, so position as much weight as possible on your feet.

Resting while climbing saves a lot of energy. It also allows your muscles to relax for a while. This helps climbers stay on the rock for longer periods of time.

Try different positions to help you rest after every few moves.

KNOTS

Different knots come in handy in different situations. The more knots you know, the better prepared you will be in an unforeseen situation. The figure-eight fol-low-through is a standard knot used to connect the rope to the harness. This type of knot is usually placed 3 feet (0.91 m) from the end of the rope. The free end is put through the harness and the figure-eight is rewoven. Other knots include the waterknot, the grapevine, and the clove hitch.

Before you start climbing crags, take some time to teach yourself how to tie a few basic knots.

GETTING A GRIP

Experienced rock climbers learn how to use several grips for many different situations. An open grip is when the hand conforms to the natural hold in the rock. The cling grip uses the fingertips to hold onto flat-topped edges or sharp microedges. The pinch grip works best on small knobs and is used when there is no available edge to hold. The wrap grip is often used on rounded, knob-like holds. In this position, nearly the entire hand is touching the rock—making it one of the most secure grips.

The kind of grip you use as you ascend a crag depends on whether the rock is sheer or knobby.

CRACK CLIMBING

Crack climbs might be necessary when there are no knobs on the rock. Imagine that a steep rock has a single, narrow crack running down part of it. You would place your fingers in this crack, with your thumbs down. You'd then turn your foot sideways and put that into the crack, too. Sometimes there's not enough room for your feet in a finger crack. It's important to study the crack's width carefully before attempting to stick your foot inside.

Hand and fist cracks are a bit wider than finger cracks. Chimney cracks will fit your whole body. When crack climbing, you may want to apply cloth athletic tape to the backs of your hands to protect against nasty abrasions.

ALTITUDE

The higher you climb, the thinner the air gets. Thin air refers to air that contains less oxygen than the air we normally breathe. Less oxygen in the air can make breathing very difficult. Once your climb exceeds 8,000 feet (about 2,400 m), the altitude change will start to affect you. Your body will need time to adjust. If you try to push yourself too hard, you may wind up with a bad case of altitude sickness. Don't be in a rush to finish your climb; take your time between moves. Also, be sure to drink a lot of fluids. Following these steps will help ease your body into the thin air.

COMPETITIVE CLIMBING

Rock climbing is not really considered a competitive sport. Nevertheless, some climbers like to compete with one another. They like to see who can climb the highest, the fastest, and the hardest routes. Real competitions are usually done outdoors—but on artificial walls. Artificial walls are used so that no climber has the advantage of having already practiced the route. The walls are often waterproofed in order to be used safely if they get wet. They are often set up in a place where large audiences can enjoy watching the climbers.

These talented climbers must follow certain rules. They are judged on how far they can climb on a pre-set route. First there are a few elimination rounds to narrow down the number of competitors. After these initial rounds, top scorers climb a new, more difficult route. If a climber falls, his or her competition is over.

Every year, a World Cup event is held to determine champions in a variety of categories. This World Cup event started in the late 1980s. Many local gyms offer their own competitive events. There are also plenty of outdoor bouldering contests to be found.

Artificial walls level the playing field at climbing competitions.

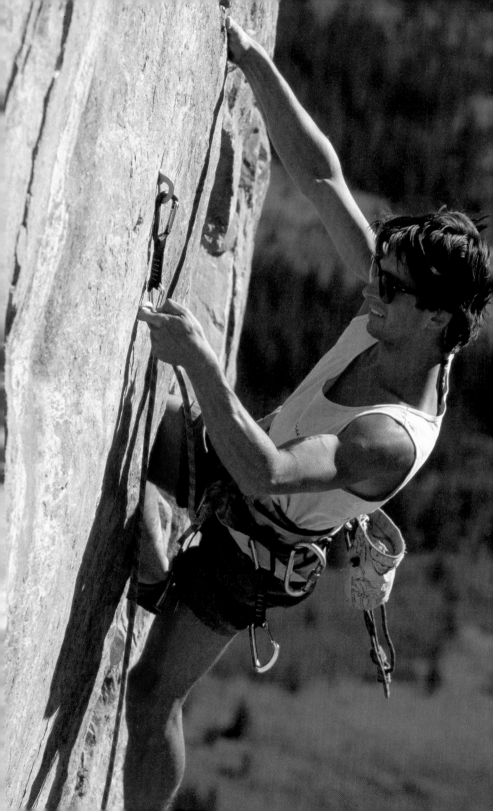

CHAPTER FOUR

CLIMB THE CRAG

Now you're familiar with basic climbing techniques. You've bought the necessary gear, and you're in great shape. You're ready to start climbing. The only thing left to do is find a crag. That's no problem—as long as you live in a rocky area. If you're not surrounded by mountains, though, there's no need to worry. You might be able to find an alternative right down the street.

Many gyms have indoor climbing walls. Indoor walls provide a safe environment to gain practice and experience. Making your first climbs in a controlled environment can prepare you for problems you might come across on a real rock.

If only the outdoors will do, plan a rock climbing vacation with your family. Study the history and

An exciting rock climbing location may only be a stone's throw away from you.

Let your rock climbing adventures take you to some of nature's most exotic settings, such as Devil's Tower in Wyoming.

geography of the mountain you plan to conquer. Doing your homework before going will help you get the most out of the adventure.

Having trouble deciding which mountain to tackle? Here are some of the nation's most popular spots:

- Yosemite National Park, California — Mountaineers from all over the world come to conquer these crags.
- Smith Rock, Oregon — Smith Rock is home to one of the nation's most difficult routes, Just Do It.

- Boulder, Colorado — Boulder has a rich climbing history. It would take an entire book to talk about all the great crags you can find here.
- Heuco Tanks, Texas — Thanks to the warm weather of the Lone Star State, this is a great place to climb during winter months.
- Devil's Tower National Monument, Wyoming — This tower is made of columns of volcanic rock. It offers steep climbs surrounded by prairie lands.
- New River Gorge, West Virginia — New River Gorge boasts over 1,200 routes. This site features 4 miles (6.4 kilometers) of sandstone, known as the Endless Wall.

ARMED WITH WILLPOWER

Mark Wellman is a great example of someone who defied the odds. A tragic climbing fall left Wellman paralyzed below the waist. Amazingly, Wellman didn't let his disability stop him from climbing. Seven years after his accident, Wellman scaled El Capitan—a 3,000-foot (0.91-km) granite face in Yosemite National Park! Wellman's amazing triumph was even televised. He now depends solely on arm strength to keep him climbing.

SIGNING UP

If you're serious about rock climbing, enroll in a class! That's right—there are a number of climbing schools across the United States and Canada. The American Mountain Guides Association can help you locate a school near your home.

Magazines also provide climbers with great information. *Climbing* and *Rock and Ice* both focus on the great outdoors. They print articles on a variety of subjects, such as new climbing techniques and great places to climb. They help their readers find good deals on gear, too.

Rock climbing is a rewarding sport. It can provide countless hours of excitement. Plus, it's a fantastic way to enjoy nature's marvels. What are you waiting for? Pack up your rack and get out there!

Rock climbers must work extremely hard to reach the tops of crags. Yet the view from the summit makes it all worthwhile.

NEW WORDS

anchors solid points of attachment to the rock, either natural, such as trees, or mechanical, such as metal wedges

belayer the person who holds the rope for the climber

bouldering climbing on rock close to the ground without equipment

carabiners gated aluminum snap links that connect various parts of the climbing system

crag a steep, rugged rock

cross training exercising both with weights and aerobically to get in shape

NEW WORDS

excursion a short journey, often to a place of interest

ligaments tough bands of tissue that connect bones

mountaineering the sport of scaling mountains

novices beginners; people who are not very experienced at doing something

regimen a plan or method often used to improve one's physical condition

terrain the physical features of land

For Further Reading

Books

Bernardy, Catherine J., and Patrick Ryan. *Rock Climbing*. Mankato, MN: Smart Apple Media, 2000.

Brimner, Larry Dane. *Rock Climbing*. Danbury, CT: Franklin Watts, 1997.

Lund, Bill. *Rock Climbing*. Mankato, MN: Capstone Press, 1996.

Magazines

Climbing
0326 Highway 133
Suite 190
Carbondale, CO 81623
(800) 493-4569

Rock & Ice
5455 Spine Road, Mezzanine A
Boulder, CO 80301
(303) 499-8410

RESOURCES

American Mountain Guides Association
710 Tenth Street, Suite 101
Golden, CO 80401
(303) 271-0984

American Alpine Club
710 Tenth Street
Golden, CO 80401
(303) 384-0110
www.americanalpineclub.org

Alpine Club of Canada
Indian Flats Road
P.O. Box 8040
Canmore, AB
T1W 2T8
(403) 678-3200

RESOURCES

Videos

Basic Rock Climbing
Vertical Adventures Productions
3200 Wilshire Boulevard
Los Angeles, CA 90010

Performance Rock Climbing—The Video
1478 East Logan
Salt Lake City, UT 84105

Web Sites

American Mountain Guides Association (AMGA)
www.amga.com

Climber.Org
www.climber.org

American Safe Climbing Association (ASCA)
www.safeclimbing.org

INDEX

INDEX

About the Author

Aileen Weintraub is a freelance author and editor living in the scenic Hudson Valley of upstate New York. She has published over thirty young adult and children's books. She edits historical manuscripts and college textbooks and works part time for a not-for-profit organization serving kids with special needs.